The Love Dare Bible Study

MICHAEL CATT

ALEX KENDRICK

STEPHEN KENDRICK

As developed with Matt Tullos

LifeWay Press®
Nashville, Tennessee

Published by LifeWay Press®. © 2009 Sherwood Baptist Church
Seventh Printing November 2010

ISBN 978-1-4158-6655-9 • Item 005186345

Dewey Decimal Classification: 220.07
Subject Heading: BIBLE--STUDY / LOVE / MARRIAGE

To order additional copies of this resource: WRITE LifeWay Church Resources Customer Service,
One LifeWay Plaza; Nashville, TN 37234-0113; FAX order to (615) 251-5933; PHONE 1-800-458-
2772; E-MAIL to orderentry@lifeway.com; ORDER ONLINE at
www.lifeway.com; or visit the LifeWay Christian Store serving you.

Printed in the United States of America

Leadership and Adult Publishing; LifeWay Church Resources;
One LifeWay Plaza; Nashville, TN 37234-0175

Contents

Session 1 • Leading Your Heart 7

Session 2 • The Power of Influence 15

Session 3 • Honoring and Cherishing Your Spouse . . 25

Session 4 • Living with Understanding 35

Session 5 • Unconditional Love 45

Session 6 • Walking in Forgiveness 55

Session 7 • Building Your Marriage on
Prayer and God's Word 65

Session 8 • Establishing a Covenant Marriage 75

Leader Guide 85

Christian Growth Study Plan 96

About the Authors

MICHAEL CATT has been senior pastor of Sherwood Baptist Church, Albany, Georgia, since 1989. In that role, he served as Executive Producer for Sherwood Pictures' films FLYWHEEL, FACING THE GIANTS, and FIREPROOF. Sherwood Pictures is the moviemaking ministry of Sherwood Baptist Church. In addition to his preaching ministry, Michael is an author, editor, and denominational leader. "We don't do any of this so people will pat us on the back. We do it for God's glory."

ALEX KENDRICK joined the staff of Sherwood in 1999 as associate minister of media, overseeing the church's television, radio, and film ministries. FIREPROOF is the third movie directed by Alex and co-written with his brother, Stephen. He also teaches a weekly televised Bible study program called Home Connection. He is a co-writer with Stephen of *The Love Dare*, a vital resource to this Bible study.

STEPHEN KENDRICK has served as associate teaching pastor/ preaching at Sherwood since 2001. Stephen and Alex helped develop Bible study resources and other tools for churches in conjunction with FACING THE GIANTS and FIREPROOF—the latter including *The Love Dare* journal, a 40-day challenge for couples to understand and practice unconditional love.

MATT TULLOS has been interpreting the truth of the gospel to youth and adults through preaching, teaching, writing, and drama ministries for 20-plus years. He has served five churches in roles of youth pastor, associate pastor, and pastor. Matt currently is pastor of Bluegrass Baptist Church, Hendersonville, Tennessee.

For more information about the movie, the church, and the authors,
visit www.fireproofthemovie.com and www.LoveDareBook.com.

About This Study

Get ready! You are about to embark on a journey, one that can provide tremendous benefit for you, your spouse, and your life together. Each week *The Love Dare Bible Study* journey will challenge you to think differently—and as a result, to learn, stretch, and grow individually and as a couple as you dare to live a life of selfless, sacrificial love.

GROUP LEADER TOOLS

• Teaching Clips DVD
• Power Truths from *The Love Dare* (CD-ROM), plus other CD articles as needed
• *The Love Dare Bible Study* member book for each attendee
• *The Love Dare* journal for each attendee
• Bibles for each attendee

COMPONENTS OF EACH SESSION

Ignite. This section includes lighthearted engaging questions designed to warm up the group and prepare them for meaningful discussion throughout the session.

Love Dare Review. Each group session (except session 1) includes a time to review the insights and benefits you may have gained as an individual or couple as you participated in *The Love Dare* during the previous week.

Gear Up. This interactive Bible study section is the heart of each group session. The goal is for the group to discover biblical truths through watching a clip from the motion picture FIREPROOF, and then allowing the Holy Spirit to guide open and engaging discussion to gain the tools necessary for godly marriages.

Firefighting. This section continues the Bible study time but with an emphasis on leading group members to integrate the truths they've discovered into their lives and to transform their marriages.

Fireproof Now. This section focuses on further application, prayer, and opportunities for you to make commitments to God and to your spouse as you work to fireproof your marriage.

Group Covenant

As your group begins this study, it is important that you discuss group values. During the first session would be the most appropriate time. It is vital that you covenant together, agreeing to live out these important principles. Once these are agreed upon, your group will be on your way to experiencing Christian community.

Priority: While we are in this course of study, we will give the group meetings and commitments to our marriages high priority.

Participation: Everyone is encouraged to participate. No one person dominates.

Respect: Everyone is given the right to his or her own opinion, and all questions are encouraged and respected. Spouses respect each other in how they respond in the group.

Confidentiality: Anything said in the meeting is never repeated outside the meeting.

Life Change: Throughout the next 8 weeks, we will assess our own life-change goals and encourage one another in our individual pursuit of becoming more like Christ.

Care and Support: Permission is given to call upon each other at any time, especially in times of crisis. The group will provide care for every member.

Accountability: We agree to let the members of the group hold us accountable to the commitments we make in whatever loving ways we decide upon.

I agree to all of the above _____

Date: _____

Leading Your Heart

SESSION 1

This study is about love, both what it is
and what it is not (1 Corinthians 13).
This experience is about
learning and daring to live a life filled
with loving relationships.

Your journey begins with the person who
is closest to you: your spouse.

Ignite

You have joined others who are on the same important journey. Introduce yourself to your fellow travelers.

"Now these three remain: faith, hope, and love. But the greatest of these is love."

1 CORINTHIANS 13:13, HCSB

1. The FIREPROOF movie is a major part of our time together. If a movie were to be made about your life, what genre would it be? Why?

❏ **Thriller** ❏ **Action/Adventure**
❏ **Drama** ❏ **Romantic Comedy**
❏ **Tragedy** ❏ **Love Story**
❏ **Horror**

Who would play you? Who would play your spouse? (No bad casting allowed!)

Humorous episodes … dramatic scenes … thrilling mysteries still unfolding—we're all in different "acts" and "scenes" in our marriages.

No matter where you are or where you think you or your spouse ought to be, you have been invited into a unique and life-changing process: a journey of exploring and demonstrating genuine love, even when your desire is dry and your motives are low.

Moment-by-moment, it seems, our culture bombards us with different messages about love.

2. In general, what do you think our society is saying to us about what love is? About following our hearts?

What phrases, titles, or situations from media (songs, movies, TV) promote the idea of following your heart?

When you think about the state of your own heart right now, circle the words that come to mind.

cold   cynical   open   joyful   weary
angry   exhilarated   other: _____

"If you have bitter jealousy and selfish ambition in your heart, do not be arrogant and so lie against the truth. This wisdom is not that which comes down from above."

JAMES 3:14-15, NASB

According to James 3:14-15 (margin) how might an angry or bitter heart take an individual (and a marriage) in the wrong direction?

Following our hearts would be good if our hearts were always loving, in tune with God and desirous of the right thing. However, since as humans we are self-centered, prideful, and often deceived, following our hearts may not always lead us to do the right thing.

"If love is just this overwhelming emotion that we can do absolutely nothing about, then no marriage is safe."

VODDIE BAUCHAM

Describe a time you followed your heart and regretted it later.

Gear Up

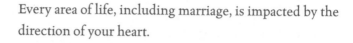

ENGAGING IN RELEVANT SCRIPTURE STUDY

MOVIE MOMENTS
Watch FIREPROOF
clip 1 "For Better or for
Worse." Debrief using
activities 3-5.

Every area of life, including marriage, is impacted by the direction of your heart.

3. In your opinion, what does Caleb Holt believe it means to be "in love"?

4. Why do you think Lieutenant Michael Simmons said, "When most people promise, 'for better or for worse', they really only mean, 'for the better'?"

Michael reminded Caleb: "That ring on your finger means you made a lifetime covenant."

5. Think back to your wedding day and the exchange of rings and vows. Were you committing to love your spouse unconditionally, for a lifetime? How's it going?

"Your heart will always be where your treasure is."
MATTHEW 6:21, CEV

Following our hearts often means chasing after whatever feels right at the moment. Our emotions and feelings can be deceptive, leading us down the wrong path. Proverbs 16:25 cautions: "There is a way that seems right to a man, but in the end it is the way of death" (HCSB).

Your heart follows your investments because your investments are those things in which you pour your time, money, and energy. It makes sense that they will draw your heart because your investments reflect your priorities.

6. **If last week was typical for you, use it to evaluate your investments. In which of these areas did you invest significant time, energy, or money? Try to recall actual percentages of time spent and related activities.**

Job

Hobby (specify)

Retirement

Spouse

Children

Church

Friends

Status/Wealth

How does your actual use of time, energy, and money match your stated priorities?

"Don't store up treasures on earth! Moths and rust can destroy them, and thieves can break in and steal them. Instead, store up your treasures in heaven, where moths and rust cannot destroy them, and thieves cannot break in and steal them."

MATTHEW 6:19-20, CEV

"If you are not in love with your spouse today, it may be because you stopped investing in your spouse yesterday."

THE LOVE DARE,
" LEADING YOUR HEART,"
PAGE 212

MOVIE MOMENTS

Watch FIREPROOF
clip 2, "Lead Your Heart."
Debrief using
activities 7 and 8.

7. Based on Michael's advice to Caleb, what had Michael learned about the heart?

"For one horrible year," Michael shared, "I got married for the wrong reasons, … and then got divorced for the wrong reasons. … I thought I was just following my heart. … You've got to lead your heart."

Leading your heart means
• Taking full responsibility for your heart's condition and direction.
• Realizing that you have control over where your heart is.
• Asking God for the power to guard or protect your heart by taking it off the wrong things and setting it on the right things.

ADDITIONAL LEADING YOUR HEART SCRIPTURES

1 Kings 8:61
Proverbs 23:17,19,26
John 14:27-28
Philippians 2:3
2 Timothy 2:22
James 4:8; 5:8

If you choose to lead your heart to invest in your spouse, then your spouse is more likely to become your treasure.

8. In the above list, circle the bulleted action(s) you will try. Pray about the italicized statement.

Love is a decision and not just a feeling. It is selfless, sacrificial, and transformational. And when love is truly demonstrated as it was intended, your relationship can change for the better.

Firefighting

COMPELLING COUPLES TO TRANSFORM THEIR MARRIAGES

Setting your heart on the right things can be a consistent commitment, not just a random attempt.

9. **If you were to put your heart under the same microscope as the psalmist David did in Psalm 139—asking God to search you and know your heart—what would you discover?**

"Search me, O God, and know my heart; test me and know my anxious thoughts. See if there is any offensive way in me, and lead me in the way everlasting."

PSALM 139:23-24, NIV

10. **From what things do you need to begin to guard your heart as the proverb recommends?**

"Above all else, guard your heart, for it is the wellspring of life."

PROVERBS 4:23, NIV

11. **What do you think the psalmist David meant in Psalm 119:112 when he determined to set his heart on God's decrees "to the very end"?**

"My heart is set on keeping your decrees to the very end."

PSALM 119:112, NIV

David was absolutely resolute, completely focused in the right direction, fully committed to following God's ways for all his life.

"Listen, my son, and be wise, And direct your heart in the way."

PROVERBS 23:19, NASB

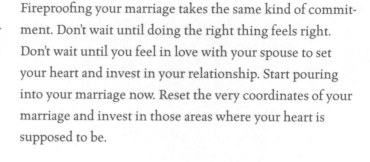

Fireproof Now

Committing Through Reflection and Prayer

"Since, then, you have been raised with Christ, set your hearts on things above."

Colossians 3:1, NIV

Fireproofing your marriage takes the same kind of commitment. Don't wait until doing the right thing feels right. Don't wait until you feel in love with your spouse to set your heart and invest in your relationship. Start pouring into your marriage now. Reset the very coordinates of your marriage and invest in those areas where your heart is supposed to be.

A Prayer for a Transformed Heart

"(Love) bears all things, believes all things, hopes all things, endures all things. Love never fails."

1 Corinthians 13:7-8 NASB

Lord Jesus, Master of our hearts,
We are desperate to see You reign in our marriages
with power and majesty.
We see the need to grow up emotionally
and become more intentional.
Lord, teach us to guard and lead our hearts
according to Your will.
This week give us the power to change old habits
and break free from old ways as we redirect
the coordinates of our hearts to You and one another.
Master of our lives, we ask for Your help and courage! Amen.

Living the Love Dare This Week

As you begin *The Love Dare* readings this week, read:
Introduction and Days 1-5
Appendix 4 (give particular attention)

The Power of Influence

SESSION 2

If you are not leading your heart, then
someone or something else is. The people
you listen to and the influences you allow
into your life impact your very
destiny as a couple.

Ignite

OPENING THOUGHTS AND CONVERSATION STARTERS

1. Enjoy letting your group get a glimpse of the story of your life and marriage.

    How did you meet your mate?

    What's one crazy thing you have done as a couple?

    Is there a couple whose marriage you admire?

YOUR LOVE DARES IN ACTION

"*Therefore, submit to God. But resist the Devil, and he will flee from you.*"

JAMES 4:7, HCSB

Days 1-5 in *The Love Dare* challenged you to live in kindness and patience with each other.

2. **What was the most significant result of your Love Dare experience last week?**

   How challenging was it "to demonstrate patience and to say nothing negative to your spouse at all"?

If the past week challenged you, realize that you have an enemy who detests your choosing to participate in this journey of demonstrating genuine love. You also have a God whose power is greater and who will honor your commitment to your marriage.

Love requires thoughtfulness on both sides—the kind of thoughtfulness that builds bridges through the constructive combination of patience, kindness, and selflessness. Love teaches us how to meet in the middle, to respect and appreciate how our spouse uniquely thinks.

Would you be surprised to discover that the success of your marriage is directly related to the influences around you? Let's look together at both the positive and negative influences on our lives and our love.

3. **It is hard to grow a rose in a house fire! How does the metaphor of a fire out of control reflect the state of many marriages today?**

> "A woman is like a rose. If you treat her right, she'll bloom. If you don't, she'll wilt."
> MICHAEL IN FIREPROOF

How does our culture make it difficult to succeed in marriage?

Which of these influences pose the greatest threat to marriages today?

Fire Hazards

_____ Media/Internet   _____ Money/debt
_____ Relationships   _____ Schedules
_____ Work   _____ Other:
_____ Recreation

Which ones also have potential for positive impact on relationships?

Gear Up

MOVIE MOMENTS
Watch FIREPROOF
clip 3 "He Said, She Said/
Phone Call." Debrief
using activity 4.

As we look at Caleb and Catherine's marriage, try to answer for yourself, *Who or what is whispering in my ear?*

4. **What influences do you observe from Catherine's conversation with her friends? From Caleb's phone call to his father? In the movie description that follows, circle the positive influences and underline the negative influences for each spouse.**

"Not everyone has the material to be a good friend. … In fact, anyone who undermines your marriage does not deserve to be given the title of "friend."
THE LOVE DARE, DAY 23

In these and other scenes in FIREPROOF, Caleb and Catherine are pulling away from each other. Once Catherine was bolstered by her mother's counsel; now that support is gone. Harsh words, anger, and disrespect characterize her treatment of Caleb. The pressure of friends pull Catherine away from Caleb and push her to consider divorce. Gavin represents all that seems to be lacking in Caleb, as Catherine takes gradual steps away from Caleb toward someone else.

Caleb's father (and mother) encourage and pray for him. Buying the boat is a higher priority to Caleb than his wife. In a high-pressure, dangerous job, Caleb finds a true friend in Michael. Michael's words and marriage are testimony to a redemptive, godly marriage. Caleb's anger, along with his Internet addiction, intensifies.

The Love Dare is part of what helped Caleb realize his need for God—and understand the only way he can love his wife unconditionally.

Well-meaning friends, in an attempt to look out for what is best for us, can provide strong negative influence. Even some of Jesus' friends, out of love for Him, tried to talk Him out of going to the cross!

Are your closest friends champions for or enemies of your marriage? Anyone who undermines your marriage does not deserve to be called a friend. Choose your friends carefully.

> Hey Dan
> Thought I'd send you this e-mail because I know you are going through some pretty difficult stuff. I know you're committed to marriage but if you are that unhappy, maybe you should just go ahead and divorce. I know you're concerned about your kids, but remember kids go through the divorces of parents and turn out fine.
>
> Plus, if you really want to help them, you are going to have to find your joy, and it certainly seems like there's no joy in your marriage. Just some friendly advice …

"The Devil is a liar and the father of liars."
JOHN 8:44, HCSB

5. **What lies about marriage has the friend in this e-mail bought into?**

MORE ON POWER OF INFLUENCE
Proverbs 1:10-15
Proverbs 27:12
Ecclesiastes 4:5-7
Matthew 5:29
1 Corinthians 12:2
Acts 9:31

6. **According to Proverbs 20:8, "A king sitting on a throne to judge sifts out all evil with his eyes." How does this proverb encourage a wise spouse to respond to negative influences in marriage?**

This proverb contrasts wisdom with foolishness. A wise spouse is able to recognize influences that could harm his or her marriage and quickly divert attention from them ("sift out all evil with his eyes"). While some influences are easy to spot, others are much more challenging to recognize.

> 7. **Now look at your own situation. As spouses, list the positive and negative influences on your marriage. (Also look back at pp. 17-18.)**

	Positive Influences	Negative Influences
Husband		
Wife		

FOR HELP,
CONSIDER
THESE VERSES...
Titus 2:2-3
Proverbs 31

> **In the "He Said/She Said" clip, Caleb told Michael, "Our marriage has been fine until this year." Do you believe this to be true? Why or why not?**

Caleb and Catherine's marriage had actually been eroding for some time, even though they were not aware. Genesis 3:1-6 remind us of Satan's cunning, of how he often uses subtlety to turn a spark of influence into an outright blaze!

Satan still whispers in our ears, "It won't hurt you"; "Did God really say that? He didn't mean it" and "No one will ever know." The enemy uses his knowledge of God and Scripture to plant doubts and to entice us in wrong directions.

8. **What subtle sparks of negative influence did you identify in activity 7? Do any have potential to become a roaring fire? List them on the sign below.**

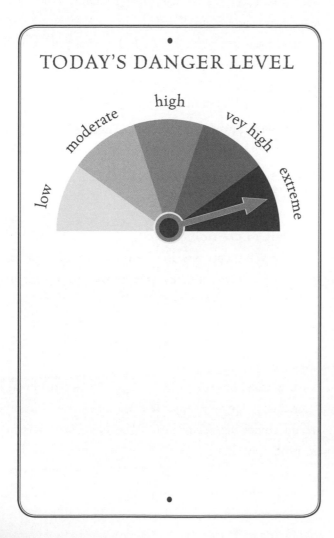

TODAY'S DANGER LEVEL

low · moderate · high · vey high · extreme

YOUR FIRE ESCAPE

"No temptation has overtaken you except what is common to humanity. God is faithful and He will not allow you to be tempted beyond what you are able, but with the temptation He will also provide a way of escape."

1 Corinthians 10:13, HCSB

Firefighting

COMPELLING COUPLES TO TRANSFORM THEIR MARRIAGES

> "You must guard yourself against the wrong influencers. Everyone has an opinion and some people will encourage you to act selfishly and leave your mate in order to pursue your own happiness. Be careful about listening to advice from people who don't have a good marriage themselves."
>
> THE LOVE DARE, DAY 35

Recognizing the sparks that threaten to burn down our marriages is one thing. Extinguishing the blaze is something entirely different. It is critical that we pursue godly advice, healthy friendships, and experienced mentors to benefit from the wisdom they have gained through their own successes and failures.

Proverbs 13:20 (HCSB) tells us, "The one who walks with the wise will become wise, but a companion of fools will suffer harm." Who is qualified to speak into *your* marriage? How do you filter *your* friends?

Couple Questions:

• **What couples do we know who bring a strong, positive mentoring influence to our marriage?**

• **What couple could we connect with to strengthen our marriage?**

Gaining wise counsel is like having a detailed road map and a personal guide on a long, challenging journey. It can mean the difference between continual success or the destruction of another marriage.

Fireproofing your marriage is about embracing the power of influence by resisting the negative hazards and inviting the positive influences to speak truth into your life and marriage. This is one way you choose to lead your heart. When you do, you safeguard your covenant relationship and your marriage becomes a positive influence to others.

COMMITTING THROUGH REFLECTION AND PRAYER

9. If you were to express a personal commitment based on the word *love*, what might it look like? Check an action that reflects your heart's desire.

Lord, as I ask for godly influence to fireproof my marriage, I choose to…

___ *L*ove my spouse by …
   choosing to listen to godly wisdom and the Word of God.

___ *O*bey God by …
   making wise choices regarding friends, mentors, and companions in the workplace, in recreation and other settings.

___ *V*alue my marriage by …
   believing that God will honor my choice to stay within the covenant of marriage and by spending time and effort to make my marriage one that can influence others in a positive way.

___ *E*xpress these truths by …
   continuing in this love dare journey and valuing this time of renewal and challenge.

A Prayer for Godly Influence

Father God,
I pray that Your voice will be so prominent an influence
that my mind, will, and emotions will desire to relentlessly
pursue a God-honoring marriage.

I confess that my heart is easily influenced by lesser voices.
So give me an unfailing desire for Your ways, not mine.
Help me to seek Your truth, not a false, deceptive counterfeit.

Bring people into my life who will guide me
into a deeper love for You and my spouse. Amen.

Living the Love Dare This Week

As you take a look at the next five love dares, continue
to take action! Encourage others in your group;
initiate conversations and e-mails during the week;
and pray for yourself, your spouse, and other couples.

Most of all, join God in His work to strengthen
marriages and see what happens. Live the dare!

Next week in *The Love Dare* read and do:
Days 6-10

Honoring and Cherishing Your Spouse

SESSION 3

Learning to rein in negative thoughts
about your spouse and focus instead on
his or her positive attributes will help you
honor your marriage in your heart.

As you begin to place your marriage under
the shade of God's unconditional love,
His love will become
your kind of love.

Ignite

OPENING THOUGHTS AND CONVERSATION STARTERS

The footprints of the past often show up in the present. Even after many years, most of us vividly recall moments of rejection and fear as well as times of joy and honor.

1. Who was your greatest hero growing up?

Do you recall ever honoring or dishonoring someone in your heart?

"Nobody can acquire honor by doing what is wrong."

THOMAS JEFFERSON

YOUR LOVE DARES IN ACTION

The apostle Paul described love as "the most excellent way" (1 Cor. 12:31, NIV). We honor our mates with our unconditional love. As a couple, read these contemporary descriptors of love.

Love accepts the pain of the relationship.
Love listens to her anger.

Love smiles when she sees him.
Love is him looking deeply in return.

Love shares intimacy through contact, both verbal and physical.
Love doesn't brag about the weight loss in front of the mate who needs to lose some weight herself.

Love doesn't parade her talent in front of his inability.
Love doesn't remember all his past exploits and victories
to make her feel lucky that he even sticks around.

Love doesn't complain about his wife.
Love doesn't rejoice in seductive images on TV.

Love believes in her husband and wants the best
for him.
Love never gives up.

2. **How did you do with the lists you created this**
   week? (Days 6 and 7)

   Can you think of a time you experienced
   the blessing of your spouse when you didn't
   deserve it?

   Share a positive attribute of your spouse that
   could be written on the walls of your Apprecia-
   tion Room. (Day 7)

Gear Up

ENGAGING IN RELEVANT SCRIPTURE STUDY

Honor can be defined as holding someone in high esteem, viewing someone or something as rare or special. In contrast, antonyms, or opposites, include words like *shame, despise* or *despising, caring little for something,* and *disrespect.*

> "When they speak to you, you take them seriously, giving their words weight and significance. When they ask you to do something, you accommodate them if at all possible, simply out of respect for who they are."
>
> THE LOVE DARE, DAY 15

3. Circle words in 1 Peter 3:7-8 (NIV) that describe a marriage of honor:

"Husbands, in the same way be considerate as you live with your wives, and treat them with respect as the weaker partner and as heirs with you of the gracious gift of life, so that nothing will hinder your prayers. Finally, all of you, live in harmony with one another; be sympathetic, love as brothers, be compassionate and humble."

What is one result of a husband not being considerate of his wife?

Your spouse is as much a part of you as your hand, your eyes, or your heart. Honor (or the lack of it) becomes apparent in our conversations with one another—and with God. Our words, reactions, facial expressions, and tone of voice all shout a clear message to our spouses. They cry out "You are priceless to me!" or "You are worthless to me!" In "The Big Fight" clip, watch for the message being communicated.

4. What do you think caused Caleb to explode?

MOVIE MOMENTS
Watch FIREPROOF
clip 4, "The Big Fight."
Debrief using
activity 4.

Everything in this scene screams "You're worthless to me!" What principles of honor do you think were destroyed?

MOVIE MOMENTS
Watch FIREPROOF
clip 5, "A Hero to
Everyone." Debrief
using activities 5-7.

As Caleb recovered at home, he reassures his mom that he really is OK—and lets his dad know he will not give up on his marriage. In the process of that conversation Caleb observed: "The newspaper called twice wanting an interview. It seems I'm a hero to everybody but my wife."

5. Do you know someone who went through a similar time of disappointment in marriage? Why do you think it is so easy for us to lose the respect of our spouses?

6. Rate the honor in these statements (high or low). In the margin, rewrite one statement to reflect respect and honor.

_____ "She used to love to call me. Now it seems the only time she calls is when she wants something."

_____ "My husband is so selfish! He thinks clean socks just fly from the hamper to the washer and dryer, and then back to the drawer."

_____ "Making love ... It has turned into a duty. How can I enjoy intimacy with someone who drives me crazy?"

_____ "She's a total ditz when it comes to finances. She barely knows how to write a check, much less balance a checkbook."

"²⁵Since you put away lying, Speak the truth, each one to his neighbor, because we are members of one another. ²⁶Be angry and do not sin. Don't let the sun go down on your anger, ²⁷and don't give the Devil an opportunity. ²⁹No rotten talk (emphasis added) should come from your mouth, but only what is good for the building up of someone in need, in order to give grace to those who hear."

Ephesians 4:25-27, 29 (margin) describes how "rotten talk" can become a habit, gradually eroding relationships.

7. **What should come out of our mouths instead?**

Why? (Also see Eph. 4:15 in the right margin.)

E p h e s i a n s 4:25-27,29,
h c s b

What do you think is meant by verse 27, "Don't give the Devil an opportunity"?

Are there times you are more vulnerable to saying hurtful words to your spouse?

"But speaking the truth in love, let us grow in every way into Him who is the head—Christ."

EPHESIANS 4:15, HCSB

Jesus is the perfect example of viewing people as priceless and of great value—valuable enough to die for. He related to each person through a "lens" of honor and respect.

8. **Depending on the lens you are looking through, by the way you interact, you are either telling your spouse he/she is priceless or worthless. Place a check under what you are communicating to your spouse in the areas below.**

WHAT I TELL MY SPOUSE ...	You Are Priceless!	You Are Worthless!
with my words		
by how I treat his/her body		
through meeting his/her needs		
by how I make requests		
with my behavior in conflict		
by keeping my commitments		

The Bible tells husbands to love their wives in the same way Christ loved the church (Eph. 5:25). When you love and honor your spouse, you are honoring and respecting Christ. The opposite is also the case.

COMPELLING COUPLES TO TRANSFORM THEIR MARRIAGES

WORDS/ACTIONS TO AVOID IN CONFLICT:

- "Always"
- "Never"
- "You" statements
- Name calling
- Demands
- Threat

"Let marriage be held in honor (esteemed worthy, precious, of great price, and especially dear) in all things. And thus let the marriage bed be undefiled (kept undishonored); for God will judge and punish the un-chaste [all guilty of sexual vice] and adulterous."

HEBREWS 13:4,
THE AMPLIFIED BIBLE

CONFLICT IS INEVITABLE

When you tied the knot as bride and groom, you joined not only your hopes and dreams but also your hurts, fears, imperfections, and emotional baggage. From the moment you unpacked from your honeymoon, you began the real process of unpacking another person.

"Pretty soon your mate started to slip off your lofty pedestal, and you off of theirs. The forced closeness of marriage began stripping away your public façades, exposing your private problems and secret habits. Welcome to fallen humanity" (*The Love Dare*, Day 13).

9. **How do you handle conflict in your marriage? Check all that apply.**

___ **Escapism**	___ **Loving acceptance**
___ **Denial**	___ **Sarcasm**
___ **Brutal honesty**	___ **Substance abuse**
___ **Angry attacks**	___ **Long talks**
___ **Surrender**	___ **Humble apology**

Using Hebrews 13:4 as a guide, what are some practical ways to esteem or highly value your marriage?

Fireproof Now

COMMITTING THROUGH REFLECTION AND PRAYER

HONOR RISKS TO MEET NEEDS

King David experienced the honor of his closest companions during battle: " 'Oh, that someone would get me a drink of water from the well near the gate of Bethlehem!" So the three mighty men broke through the Philistine lines, drew water from the well near the gate of Bethlehem and carried it back to David" (2 Sam. 23:15-16, NIV).

David didn't ask anyone to act but the mighty men observed and listened. With great valor and honor, at the risk of their lives, they acted to fulfill the need.

10. What do you think that kind of honor would feel and look like in your marriage?

In session 2 you were introduced to the LOVE acrostic as one means of expressing your personal commitments. In our closing time together, for now, complete "Love my spouse by ... " with your own actions.

Lord, as I ask for godly influence to fireproof my marriage, I choose to…

__ *L*ove my spouse by …

__ *O*bey God by …
lavishing honor upon my mate even when it seems difficult or irrational.

__ *V*alue my marriage by …
allowing nothing to move this covenant I've made to my spouse and to God.

__ *E*xpress these truths by …
seeking real peace and contentment, knowing true pleasure follows the one I honor.

A Prayer for a Servant Heart

Heavenly Father, I choose to make my expression of love to my mate in a way that leads to greater intimacy with You. I am powerless to do this in my own strength. I need You! Teach me, Jesus, to revel in the life of a servant. Amen.

Living the Love Dare This Week
In *The Love Dare*, experience days 11-15 for your marriage!

Living with Understanding

Session 4

We enjoy discovering as much
as we can about the things we really care
about. You are challenged to choose
to earn a lifelong doctoral degree
in the study of your spouse—
a wonderfully complex creation of God.

Ignite

"The difference between the right word and the almost right word is the difference between lightning and the lightning bug."

MARK TWAIN

1. Share a humorous story of miscommunication in your marriage. What false assumptions did you have?

Do you or your spouse have code words that mean something to you but not to anyone else?

YOUR LOVE DARES IN ACTION

This past week you were invited to read and do the love dares for days 11-15.

2. What are you learning about love?

About communication?

"*Agape* love is 'in sickness and health' love, 'for richer or poorer' love, 'for better or worse' love."

THE LOVE DARE, DAY 10

Phileo and *eros* describe the kind of love that is responsive in nature and that fluctuates based on feelings or circumstances. *Agape* love is selfless and unconditional. You are being challenged to "Agape Love" your spouse.

The Bible tells us, "In this is love, not that we loved God, but that He loved us and sent His Son to be the propitiation for our sins" (1 John 4:10, NASB). God doesn't love us because we are lovable but because He is so loving. Unconditional love is God's kind of love.

A METAPHOR THAT'S TOO REAL

Some days life seems like a jigsaw puzzle. We try to put it all together but all we see are seemingly unconnected pieces.

3. A talk show host once had a segment called "Things that make you go *Hmm* …."
   What one thing about your spouse makes you go *Hmm* … ?

   What do you think leads to misunderstandings in marriage?

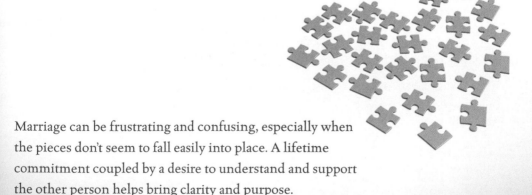

Marriage can be frustrating and confusing, especially when the pieces don't seem to fall easily into place. A lifetime commitment coupled by a desire to understand and support the other person helps bring clarity and purpose.

Gear Up

ENGAGING IN RELEVANT SCRIPTURE STUDY

MOVIE MOMENTS
Watch FIREPROOF
clip 6, "Study Your
Spouse." Debrief using
activity 4.

The Holy Spirit was at work in Caleb's life through *The Love Dare*. Watch the FIREPROOF clip for insights that began to impact Caleb's relationship with Catherine.

Then think about your answers to these questions: *Do I know my spouse's greatest hopes and dreams? Do I fully understand, how he or she prefers to give and receive love? Do I know my spouse's greatest fears and why they are a struggle?*

4. **Based on what you know about your spouse's likes and dislikes, what degree do you hold in your marriage?**

   ___ **A master's degree**
   ___ **A doctorate**
   ___ **A GED**
   ___ **I'm in remedial studies.**

Don't you enjoy discovering new things about your hobbies, passions, and interests? Of course you do! Make the same highly valued practice a part of your discovery of the most important person in your life.

A Portrait of Compassion

The first chapter of Mark (1:40-45) presents us with an incredible picture of Jesus. Here Jesus encountered a leper. In the first century a leper was considered an outcast of outcasts, a reject who not only suffered a horrible skin disease but also debilitating loneliness. Yet, in this setting, when "a leper came to Jesus" (NASB), the Lord showed compassion to him.

In the original language, the word *compassion* doesn't mean to feel sorry for a person. It doesn't mean pity, as some would imagine. Even the word *empathy* falls short. The word *compassion* means to actually get in the middle of the mess. Jesus was moved to take on the burden of the leper.

Jesus doesn't just want to connect physically or emotionally with us. He desires to be in the middle of the wreck.

5. Can you recall a time you seemed to physically feel your spouse's pain?

DIG DEEPER

2 Kings 13:23

Nehemiah 9:27

Psalm 103:13

Isaiah 54:8

In any marriage, there is no passion without compassion.

"A wise man will hear and increase in learning, And a man of understanding will acquire wise counsel."

PROVERBS 1:5, NASB

A person's heart is a guarded vault of priceless treasure. People tend to only open their hearts up to those with whom they feel emotionally safe and can completely trust. Is the heart of your spouse an open door to you or a closed wall?

6. **Why do you think it is so hard for some people to ask for help from their mates? Check any attitudes that might contribute to this barrier.**

_____ **When I ask for something, I feel less independent.**

_____ **My spouse should be more perceptive and know what I need without my having to ask.**

_____ **I've tried to ask for things but always seem to be disappointed so I've stopped asking.**

_____ **I'm afraid she will hold it over my head if I ask for something.**

Is there anything you need from your spouse that you have not yet verbalized?

GOD WANTS MORE FROM US

"But God demonstrates his own love for us in this: While we were still sinners, Christ died for us." *Romans 5:8,* NIV

The world's system proclaims that if someone wrongs you, then payback is coming hard and heavy. Our sinful nature causes us to retaliate. Yet God wants more from us!

"'An eye for an eye' religion? Not with Me," Jesus said many times in words and in action. Jesus' example of mercy and grace is foundational to living with understanding.

Firefighting

COMPELLING COUPLES TO TRANSFORM THEIR MARRIAGES

LEARN, LEARN, LEARN

"Wise men store up knowledge, But with the mouth of the foolish, ruin is at hand." *Proverbs 10:14,* NASB

The salt and pepper analogy in FIREPROOF is a great reminder of the uniquenesses of men and women—differences God has ordained since creation.

7. Which perceived differences between men and women have you experienced personally?

The Lost Wallet

She was frustrated that I had lost my wallet. Again.

She's so organized and rarely loses anything. I must have walked around the block five times. *Why does she make me this crazy? Why can't I handle this?*

As I walked, I kept hearing, *You lose everything! Why can't you grow up and take responsibility for things! You are still a dumb scatterbrained, ADD kid. You'll never change!*

I began to realize it wasn't my wife's voice that was ringing in my ear; it was my dad's. Years of his constant frustration with me came back with a vengeance. Then I realized that this incident (the lost wallet) was really about that (a wounded child).

8. What harmful baggage have you carried into your marriage that needs to be cast out? Does your spouse understand its impact on you?

FOR FURTHER READING

- *The Five Love Languages,*
  Gary Chapman
- *The DNA of Relationships,*
  Gary Smalley
- *Captivating,*
  Stasi Eldredge and
  John Eldredge
- *Wild at Heart,*
  John Eldredge
- *For Men Only* and
  For Women Only,
  Shaunti Feldhahn

LISTEN FIRST

"My dearly loved brothers, understand this: everyone must be quick to hear, slow to speak, and slow to anger."
James 1:19, HCSB

9. **Practice by turning to your spouse and asking, "What is one thing that causes you concern in our lives?"**

LISTENING TIPS
Your spouse wants to know you are listening. Sometimes that means to *not*
• give advice.
• try to "fix it."
• defend your view.
• even apologize until your spouse knows you have fully heard.

At the appropriate time, repeat what you have heard.

How difficult was it to listen without responding or trying to "fix it"?

SHOW RESPECT

"Husbands, in the same way be considerate as you live with your wives, and treat them with respect as the weaker partner and as heirs with you of the gracious gift of life, so that nothing will hinder your prayers." *1 Peter 3:7,* NIV

10. **How can you assert respect for your spouse's ...**

Time?

Needs?

Body?

Emotions?

Fireproof Now

COMMITTING THROUGH REFLECTION AND PRAYER

Prayerfully express your *Obey* action in such a way that you show compassion toward your spouse.

Lord, as I ask for godly influence to fireproof my marriage, I choose to…

__ *L*ove my spouse by …
listening, really listening to what my helpmate is saying without immediately defending my own actions or judging.

__ *O*bey God by …

"God, who knows secrets about us that we even hide from ourselves, loves us at a depth we cannot begin to fathom. How much more should we—as imperfect people— reach out to our spouse in grace and understanding, … assuring them that their secrets are safe with us?"
THE LOVE DARE, DAY 17

__ *V*alue my marriage by …
discovering new ways to love my spouse so that I show complete devotion to him/her.

__ *E*xpress these truths by …
ordering my life to facilitate closeness in communication, physical touch, gifts, recreation, and intimacy and affection.

A PRAYER FOR UNDERSTANDING

Lord Jesus, my Designer and King,
I pray for divine insight and inspiration in my life.
Give me the discernment I need to bless my family and spouse.
Teach us both to live by faith, having the ability to navigate
through difficult issues and hard times.

Give us communication that isn't just surface talk. Help us
to spend our words wisely and listen with a heart of compassion.

You brought us together. You claimed us.
And we claim each other for the glory of Your Kingdom. Amen.

LIVING THE LOVE DARE THIS WEEK

This week in your *The Love Dare* readings, you will
be challenged further to become a true scholar of
your mate's needs, desires, and passions.

This week in *The Love Dare* read and do:
Days 16-20

Unconditional Love

SESSION 5

You cannot give what you do not have.
You must have the love of Christ
before you can truly give unconditional
love to anyone else.
Christ's love is not based on merit,
circumstance, or consequence. We are
to have a relationship with our spouse
that relentlessly, stubbornly,
sacrificially loves.

OPENING THOUGHTS AND CONVERSATION STARTERS

1. When you entered the room today, someone gave you a gift. How did this make you feel? What did you do to deserve it?

   Can you recall another time when someone gave you a "no-strings-attached" gift?

YOUR LOVE DARES IN ACTION

This past week you were invited to read and do the love dares for days 16–20.

2. Day 16 challenged you to pray for your spouse's heart. As you feel comfortable, share one of the ways you are praying for your mate.

   How does praying for your spouse change your view of your marriage?

Did you find time for a special dinner together (Day 18)? If so, share about it briefly.

Every couple experiences moments in marriage when love seems to fade. Life can beat us up at times, whether through a disappointing year or the death of someone we hold dear. In the midst of storms, couples may find themselves either pulling together or pulling away from each other.

We can lead our hearts to choose love. Yet, at the same time, the kind of love we need—love that is able to withstand every kind of pressure—is beyond our reach. We need someone who can give us that kind of love.

God is your source for unconditional love. As you walk with Him, He can give you a love for your spouse that you could never produce on your own. He wants to love your spouse through you.

The Bible clearly tells us, "God is love. When we take up permanent residence in a life of love, we live in God and God lives in us" (1 John 4:16, The Message). Allow those words to absorb you, to go down deep within you—much deeper than Sunday songs and bumper-sticker slogans.

God is love, and His love is unconditional. He's not a cosmic commando ready to fire spiritual missiles at you every time you mess up. God is not the enemy. He loves you. He is for you. And if you have never reached out to Him, know He has been reaching out to you your entire life.

"⁷Beloved, let us love one another, for love is from God; and everyone who loves is born of God and knows God. ⁸The one who does not love does not know God, for God is love. ⁹By this the love of God was manifested in us, that God has sent His only begotten Son into the world so that we might live through Him."

1 JOHN 4:7-9, NASB

3. **When have you felt the complete and total love of God?**

In difficult times, do you and your spouse tend to cling to each other or claw at each other?

Gear Up

ENGAGING IN RELEVANT SCRIPTURE STUDY

MOVIE MOMENTS
Watch FIREPROOF
clip 7, "Trust Him with
Your Life." Debrief
using activity 4.

"I've bent over backwards
for (Catherine). I've tried
to demonstrate that I
still care about this
relationship.… I've
taken her insults and
sarcasm. But last night
was it. I did everything
I could to demonstrate
that I care about her, to
show value for her and
she spat in my face! How
am I supposed to show
love to somebody over
and over and over who
constantly rejects me?"

CALEB TO HIS FATHER
IN FIREPROOF

4. **In this scene, where is Caleb coming from
regarding his view of God and salvation?**

**Why do you think Catherine is so unresponsive
to Caleb's attempts to complete *The Love Dare*?**

**How does the cross change our perspective
about love?**

"God demonstrates his own love for us in this: While we were still sinners, Christ died for us (*Rom. 5:8*, NIV). This is how we know what love is. Jesus Christ came to "seek and to save" *you* and *me* (*Luke 19:10*).

Jesus places a high commodity on love! His command (and example) to *Love one another* is a command that is above and beyond any commandment before or since.

Jesus tossed the old self-preserving, me-first mind-set and calls us to be the most passionate, curiously peculiar lovers that the world has ever known. He taught: "Love your enemies. Help and give without expecting a return" (*Luke 6:35*, The Message).

His is the kind of love that makes a practice and a lifestyle of unconditional love. Such love goes deeper than appeasing, compromising, and tolerating. It runs beyond treaties, borders, and time limits. This love is a powerful, courageous love. It is putting skin and bones on this life called *Christianity*. Unconditional love endures. It hopes. It believes.

In other words, don't just practice this radical mission of unconditional love on the good days when the car works, the garbage has been taken out, and the kids are sweet and admirable. Don't just camp out in the wilderness of love. Build your home there.

"I give you a new commandment: love one another. Just as I have loved you, you must also love one another. "

JOHN 13:34, HCSB

"(Love) always protects, always trusts, always hopes, always perseveres. Love never fails."

1 CORINTHIANS 13:7-8, NIV

5. **Everyone has been touched by the pain and tragedy of divorce. In situations you know about, what was the major cause?**

___ Addictions	___ Abuse	___ Infidelity
___ Finances	___ Illness	___ Anger
___ Lies	___ Boredom	___ Other

"²I know your works, your labor, and your endurance, and that you cannot tolerate evil. You have tested those who call themselves apostles and are not, and you have found them to be liars. ³You also possess endurance and have tolerated many things because of My name, and have not grown weary. ⁴But I have this against you: you have abandoned the love you had at first."

REVELATION 2:2-4, HCSB

"For I am persuaded that neither death nor life, nor angels nor rulers, nor things present, nor things to come, nor powers, nor height, nor depth, nor any other created thing will have the power to separate us from the love of God that is in Christ Jesus our Lord!"

ROMANS 8:38-39, HCSB

Does unconditional love give up when things get tough? How does love respond, instead, to help heal these issues?

ATTRIBUTES OF UNCONDITIONAL LOVE

Unconditional love is steady and relentless.

6. In Revelation 2:2-4, Jesus speaks to the church at Ephesus about love. What is He saying about the relationship of His bride (the church) to Himself?

Unconditional love is binding and unifying.

Read Romans 8:38-39 (margin).

Unconditional love goes above and beyond reasonable expectations.

Unconditional love is a rare commodity these days. People love when they receive love. They love when they are treated as lovely.

However, unconditional love isn't bartered love, traded on the open market. It is the kindness of the Samaritan who ministers to a beaten man whose nature is to despise him. Love is a woman at the end of her desperate rope, breaking and pouring her life savings to honor the life of her friend. Love is offering dying mercy to a criminal in his final hour—the last person to whom you would want to extend kindness and hope and grace.

7. **Read the Parable of the Prodigal Son in your Bible (Luke 15:11-32). Who are the main characters?**

   Who personifies conditional love?

   Who personifies unconditional love?

8. **How can you best communicate unconditional love to your spouse?**

   When he or she fails?

   When he or she seems unlovable?

   When you feel like giving up?

Remember your vows! When you married, did you vow to love your spouse when you felt like it; or in sickness and in health, for richer and for poorer, for better or for worse?

COMPELLING COUPLES TO TRANSFORM THEIR MARRIAGES

"²²*Wives, submit to your own husbands as to the Lord,* ²³*for the husband is head of the wife as also Christ is head of the church. He is the Savior of the body.* ²⁴*Now as the church submits to Christ, so wives should submit to their husbands in everything.* ²⁵*Husbands, love your wives, just as also Christ loved the church and gave Himself for her.*"

EPHESIANS 5:22-25, HCSB

"*Just as the Father has loved Me, I have also loved you; abide in My love. If you keep My commandments, you will abide in My love; just as I have kept My Father's commandments and abide in His love.*"

JOHN 15:9-10, NASB

BRINGING UNCONDITIONAL LOVE HOME

A godly marriage is a metaphor of unconditional love.

9. Read Ephesians 5:22-25 (margin).

Who sacrifices in this passage?

Who serves in this passage?

Are the roles different? How?

What is more sacrificial, the wife who is called by God to respect the leadership of her imperfect husband or the husband who is called to love his imperfect wife so much he would die for her? Both require you to die to self and to put another person's needs above your wants.

This type of love is impossible apart from a close relationship with Jesus Christ. When we walk with Him on a daily basis, His Holy Spirit pours out unconditional love in our hearts (Rom. 5:1-5; Gal. 5:22). Then we can love our spouse and others with that love. Jesus modeled the servanthood required for a marriage to work, in Philippians 2:5-11, As you look over this passage, you will see Him consistently put the needs of others above His own rights.

Fireproof Now

COMMITTING THROUGH REFLECTION AND PRAYER

As you make your personal commitments to your spouse and your marriage, do so in light of Philippians 2. Continue filling out your own LOVE acrostic, this time looking at the letter V and *Valuing Your Marriage.* What better way to value your marriage than by committing to a lifestyle of unconditional love? Use the space provided to write your commitment(s).

"He humbled himself and became obedient to death even death on a cross!"

PHILIPPIANS 2:8, NIV

Lord, as I ask for godly influence to fireproof my marriage, I choose to …

___ *L*ove my spouse by …
being accepting and open, trusting God to renew my mate into the person He has called.

___ *O*bey God by …
accepting the role of a servant toward my beloved and practicing the art of agape love.

___ *V*alue my marriage by …

___ *E*xpress these truths by …
offering love as an act of worship to God and covenant to my mate.

A PRAYER FOR SELFLESS LOVE

Lord Jesus, Son of God,
How rich is Your mercy toward me!
How amazing Your grace! In times when
I turn my back on You, You relentlessly reach out
to me. So much love, Lord Jesus.
It is hard to take it all in.

You loved me unconditionally when You broke the bread
and offered the cup of forgiveness.
Thank You, Jesus, Son of God.

Give me the courage to follow You into a selfless
love affair with my spouse. From this day forward, love my mate
through me. Amen.

LIVING THE LOVE DARE THIS WEEK

This week you will be challenged to go deeper into
a more intimate spiritual relationship with Christ
and in your partnership with your spouse. You will
be challenged to get out of your comfort zone spiritually. Take the leap! It's worth it!

**Continue your journey through *The Love Dare*
by reading and doing days 21–25.**

Walking in Forgiveness

SESSION 6

Complete forgiveness means holding
nothing between you and your spouse and
deciding, "I will make a daily commitment
to practice forgiveness as a lifestyle."

Ignite

1. Take a few minutes to share the most unusual or funny accident you have ever had.

   What was damaged?

   Were you able to laugh about it at the time? Can you laugh about it now?

   Did you have to apologize to anyone?

Accidents happen and we sometimes have to apologize for unintentional actions or outcomes. It's easy to become defensive about our actions when life seems to fall apart. You may have heard (or even said!) such things as "I apologize even though I wasn't at fault." "Look, if you want an apology, here goes: Sorry!"

YOUR LOVE DARES IN ACTION

You were challenged last week to ask God to reveal areas in which you struggle to do the right thing.

2. What did God show you?

   How did you wrestle with those areas of struggle last week?

What did you discover about the expectations you place on yourself? On your spouse? On God?

Great marriages don't happen because couples stop sinning and failing one another; that's impossible. Great marriages happen because couples learn to never stop apologizing and forgiving one another. When couples don't forgive and mercy runs out, things like this begin to happen:

> "How long do I live like this? I can't seem to do anything right. I walk on eggshells afraid that I'll mess up. And when I feel like that, I'm not able to share anything real with her. Even intimacy seems forced and cold.
>
> "Where did I go wrong? Lord, can you really give us a new start because it doesn't seem possible. We're so broken right now. Some days it seems like we're just in this thing for the kids." (Anonymous)

3. **Why do you think it is so hard for couples like this to get back to a place of romance and health in their marriages?**

Couples can reconcile even after being devastated by affairs, addictions, or "irreconcilable differences." However, there is one universal factor that is required for any marriage turn-around: COMPLETE FORGIVENESS.

Gear Up

ENGAGING IN RELEVANT SCRIPTURE STUDY

MOVIE MOMENTS
Watch FIREPROOF
clip 8, "Take All the
Time You Need."
Debrief using activity 4.

4. How has Caleb's attitude changed since he began *The Love Dare*?

What's the difference between forced apologies and the attitude Caleb expresses in this scene?

Circle the adjectives that best describe Caleb's attitude in this scene.

Showy	Insincere	Remorseful
Scared	Peaceful	Sarcastic
Flexible	Angry	Vindictive

"Catherine, I'm sorry....
I have been so selfish.
For the last seven years
I've trampled on you
with my words and my
actions. I have loved
other things when I
should have loved you.
In the last few weeks
God has given me a
love for you that I've

When it comes to apologizing, do you consider yourself strong or weak? Why?

5. How does unforgiveness affect you:

Physically?

Emotionally?

Spiritually?

Sexually?

In your relationship with your friends?

In your relationship with your kids?

never had before. I have asked Him to forgive me and I am hoping and praying that somehow you would be able to forgive me too. I do not want to live the rest of my life without you."

CALEB TO CATHERINE,
IN FIREPROOF

THE IMPACT OF UNFORGIVENESS

Unforgiveness causes bitterness and poisons every area of our lives. Physically it raises our stress level, hardens our facial features, and lowers our resistance to disease. Emotionally it makes us perpetually angry, irritable, and drained. It also is damaging spiritually.

"Whenever you stand praying, if you have anything against anyone, forgive him, so that your Father in heaven will also forgive you your wrongdoing. But if you don't forgive, neither will your Father in heaven forgive your wrongdoing" (*Mark 11:25-26*, HCSB). When Jesus commands us to forgive from our heart, He is teaching us to live the way God lives while also protecting us from the poison of bitterness.

In day 25 of *The Love Dare*, in Jesus' vivid parable of forgiveness (Matt. 18)—did you notice the denominations of money mentioned? The servant owed the king 10,000 talents, a debt he would not be able to pay in 1,000 lifetimes.

1 Denarius= 1 day's wage
1 Talent= 10 years' wage

In the same passage an acquaintance of the servant owed his peer 100 denarii, practically one-third of a man's yearly earnings.

6. **What "100-denarii" debts do we owe in our marriages?**

    What "10,000-talent" debts do we owe God?

God doesn't skimp when it comes to forgiveness! The word *forgive* can be translated "pardon." According to *Psalm 103:12*, HCSB: "As far as the east is from the west, so far has He removed our transgressions from us." God plunges our sins into the very depths of the sea: "You will again have compassion on us; you will tread our sins underfoot and hurl all our iniquities into the depths of the sea" *Micah 7:19*, NIV.

FALLACIES OF UNFORGIVENESS

7. **Read the following statements of forgiveness and discuss as a group or as couples why they simply aren't true.**

    "When I say I'm sorry, you should forget about the problem that I created."

    "You shouldn't forgive until he has first apologized and fixed his problems."

    "Since she was 'more' wrong than I was, I don't have to apologize for my 'smaller' part."

What other statements could you add?

8. Circle the results of unforgiveness you have observed in others or experienced personally.

Pain   Isolation   Hate

Anger   Irritability   Bitterness

Sickness   Rebellion   Spiritual Dryness

WHAT DOES IT MEAN TO TRULY FORGIVE SOMEONE?

Forgiveness begins when you choose to treat another person the same way you want God to treat you. It's when you extend the same undeserved mercy God extended to you through the sacrifice of His Son. Forgiveness happens when you let God be the Judge of another and release all your anger and vengeance over to Him. It means that you set the offender free from the debt they owe you and let them out of the prison of anger you have kept in your heart.

"Be kind and compassionate to one another, forgiving one another, just as God also forgave you in Christ."

EPHESIANS 4:32, HCSB

Consider making this statement a habit in your life and marriage: "I will forgive others the same way that I want God to forgive me!"

Firefighting

Compelling Couples to Transform Their Marriages

"¹³Christ has redeemed us from the curse of the law by becoming a curse for us, because it is written: 'Cursed is everyone who is hung on a tree.' ¹⁴The purpose was that the blessing of Abraham would come to the Gentiles in Christ Jesus, so that we could receive the promise of the Spirit through faith."

Galatians 3:13-14, hcsb

"(He) is able to do far more abundantly beyond all that we ask or think, according to the power that works within us."

Ephesians 3:20, nasb

Leading Your Heart to Forgive

We can begin to start putting His pattern of love and forgiveness into practice in our relationships and attitudes.

9. **Check one action you will attempt to put into practice in some area of your life next week.**

___ **Ask God to show you *why* you do what you do (Ps. 139:23).**

___ **Confess so healing can begin (Jas. 5:16).**

___ **Extend mercy and forgiveness to anyone who has hurt you (Mark 11:25). Say, "I forgive." We often carry guilt long after someone is deceased, and still need to forgive.**

___ **Receive forgiveness by accepting God's forgiveness and forgiving yourself (1 John 1:9-10).**

___ **Celebrate forgiveness with thankfulness and worship (Pss. 30; 32).**

___ **Make a commitment to never stop forgiving others (Ps. 22:22).**

The act of forgiveness begins and ends with complete surrender to Christ! As Galatians 3:13-14 and Ephesians 3:20 show (margin), when you surrender yourself to Christ, His power can work through you. Yet, even at your very best, you are not able to live up to God's standards.

But with Christ we can be freed and can forgive. *That's* how you love your spouse unconditionally.

COMMITTING THROUGH REFLECTION AND PRAYER

One way to express your commitment to walk in forgiveness is to let your spouse off the hook and accept him/her unconditionally, in the same way Christ accepts you.

It's time for you to write your own commitment in the space beneath *Express These Truths*.

Lord, as I ask for godly influence to fireproof my marriage, I choose to…

___ *L*ove my spouse by…
never allowing the sun to go down on my anger.

___ *O*bey God by…
following Christ's example of forgiveness in my marriage. I choose not to hold onto the past. I choose to forgive.

___ *V*alue my marriage by…
listening to my spouse and feeling the pain of my sin when I miss the mark. I will not defend my position but will seek to understand and take responsibility for my actions.

___ *E*xpress these truths by…

A PRAYER FOR FORGIVENESS

*Father, The greatest miracle of my life is the wideness
of Your forgiveness. I am amazed by Your love for me.*

*I admit that there are times when I have wounded
and times when I have been wounded. I pray that
the grace, love, and forgiveness that flowed down
on me, will also flow freely in my marriage.*

*Teach me how to forgive as I have been forgiven.
I pray that You will help me be the first
to initiate reconciliation in my home. Amen.*

LIVING THE LOVE DARE THIS WEEK

This week take the dare to express your love in a tangible
way to your spouse. Begin praying for inspiration and
creativity. Go all out as you live the dare!

Continue in *The Love Dare* by reading days 26-30.

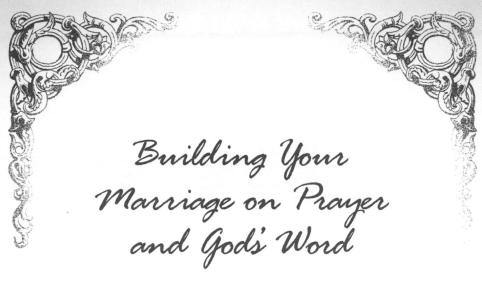

Building Your Marriage on Prayer and God's Word

SESSION 7

Marriage is God's beautiful, priceless gift.
By remaining teachable, you learn to do
the one thing that is most important
in marriage—to love (1 Cor. 13:3).

Placing all aspects of your marriage
under the authority of God's Word
and prayer is the greatest decision
for ultimate marriage success.

OPENING THOUGHTS AND CONVERSATION STARTERS

1. **What were some of your favorite meals when you were growing up?**

   What recipe disaster do you recall?

   Do any recipes for disaster exist in life?

YOUR LOVE DARES IN ACTION

This past week, in days 26-30 of *The Love Dare*, you were able to spend some time talking together about past issues.

2. **What types of issues were there? Can you share with the group any that you are facing together?**

___ Financial	___ Children
___ Communication	___ In-laws
___ Trust	___ Sexual
___ Behavior	

   What difference did it make when you gave attention to any unrealistic expectations you had been holding about your spouse? (Day 27)

Gear Up

ENGAGING IN RELEVANT SCRIPTURE STUDY

Ken:	Are you sure we can do this?
Ann:	Doug and Jane do it regularly. She says it's the best thing that's ever happened to their marriage.
Ken:	Really? That's what she says?
Ann:	You have to notice the improvement.
Ken:	So, they just walk in and say whatever's on their minds?
Ann:	Absolutely.
Ken:	What's he going to think?
Ann:	He already knows, I think.
Ken:	I feel inadequate and a little embarrassed. So, what are you going to say?
Ann:	I'm not sure. I don't know where to start either.
Ken:	Do we need to study a little more first?
Ann:	Ken, you know we need it. Let's just start.
Ken:	You're right. OK.
Ann:	Let's go.
Ken and Ann:	*"Lord, we're here."*

3. Why is it so hard for us to pray as couples?

Prayer sets our directional course and power—the light on the runway; the communication with the control tower. Yet many people, like Ken and Ann in our dialogue, don't know what prayer is or how to begin, much less tap its vast resources. Prayer is direct communication with God.

MOVIE MOMENTS
Watch FIREPROOF clip 9, "Praying at the Cross." Debrief using activity 4.

4. **In this clip, why do you think Caleb is so desperately pouring out his heart to God?**

What happens when we begin to pray for our spouses?

Describe a time when you prayed for a break- through in your marriage.

Getting Started

1. Pray for yourself
2. Pray for your spouse
3. Pray together
4. Pray with your family

Prayer works. It's a spiritual phenomenon created by an unlimited, powerful God. And it yields amazing results.

Do you feel like giving up on your marriage? Jesus said to pray instead of quitting (Luke 18:1). Are you stressed out and worried? Prayer can bring peace to your storms (Phil. 4:6–7) Do you need a major breakthrough? Prayer can make the difference (Acts 12:1-17).

Strong Buildings

The Sermon on the Mount gives us a practical guide on which to build our marriages and homes.

> 5. **Read Matthew 7:24-27. What principles from these verses apply to marriage relationships?**

Failing to build on the right foundations is both foolish and dangerous. According to *1 Samuel 12:23*, HCSB: "I vow that I will not sin against the LORD by ceasing to pray for you. I will teach you the good and right way." Samuel pointed to prayererlessness as sin against God. We should pray *for* and *with* our spouses.

Samuel's call to prayer came to Israel on the heels of a terrible threat of war by a wicked kingdom. Saul called the men to war but he was acting in self-confidence and he battled under the sole resource of his own strength. It was not enough and Samuel knew it.

We are called to cooperate with God in our personal battles. God wants us to join Him but instead we often say, "I'll fix it myself."

Prayer should be…

Authentic

Strategic

Consistent

Biblical

Unlimited

Immediate

Passionate

What words would you add as you encounter God in prayer?

Prayer does not have to be complicated or sound pious with big religious words. It can be your simply sharing honestly with God about where you are and what you are feeling and needing. Don't try to impress anyone during prayer. Just be humble and honest before God.

MOLDING US FOR HIS PURPOSES

Building on the right foundation also means spending time in God's Word, the Bible. God's Word is how He reveals Himself to us.

One of the most impressive things about the Bible is the way it is linked together, with consistent themes running throughout, from beginning to end. Although written over a span of 1,600 years and composed by more than forty writers of various backgrounds, God sovereignly authored it with one united voice. The Bible is holy, inerrant, infallible, and completely authoritative (Prov. 30:5-6; John 17:17; Ps. 119:89). God continues to speak through it to us today.

The Bible is profitable for teaching, reproving, correcting, and training in righteousness. These verses place a holy seal of approval on the Word of God for molding our lives and our marriages to Him.

> "All Scripture is inspired by God and is profitable for teaching, for rebuking, for correcting, for training in righteousness, so that the man of God may be complete, equipped for every good work."
> *2 Timothy 3:16-17*, HCSB

6. **How has the Word of God …**
   - **corrected or rebuked you over the course of your marriage?**

• *trained* you to become a godly spouse?

• *equipped* you for every good work, including to stand strong during a difficult season?

COUPLE TIME

7. Share with each other three things for which you would like the other person to begin praying for you.

What dreams for the future do you have that will require prayer?

The Bible Is the Word of God

If I …

Believe its truth, I will be set free (John 8:32).

Hide it in my heart, I will be protected in times of temptation (Ps. 199:11).

Continue in it, I will become a true disciple (John 8:31).

Meditate on it, I will become successful (Josh. 1:8).

Keep it, I will be rewarded and my love perfected (Ps. 19:7-11; 1 John 2:5).

FROM "THE WORD OF GOD IN MY LIFE," PAGES 208-09, THE LOVE DARE

Husbands and wives bring their own cultural traditions and family habits into marriage. They have ideas about how their new home should operate. The most unifying practice is to filter all these traditions and ideas through the Word of God and let its voice bring direction for how they live as a couple and as a family.

Firefighting

COMPELLING COUPLES TO TRANSFORM THEIR MARRIAGES

TEST YOUR FAMILY INFLUENCES

Continuing as couples, do this exercise separately and talk about your answers together. In the blanks below, write the letter(s) that represent sources of strong influence on each area of your marriage and family life. For example, if your views on roles are based on what your parents believed, write the letter F.

C - Culture

F - Family Traditions

P - Personal Preferences

G - God's Word

Family values/priorities: _____

Family goals/directions: _____

Roles of husband and wife: _____

Our view of marriage: _____

How we work through conflict: _____

Child-rearing: _____

Financial decisions: _____

Our sexual relationship: _____

COMMITTING THROUGH REFLECTION AND PRAYER

As you write out your commitments here, be assured that prayer and God's Word are your power source to accomplish those commitments, not just to your spouse, but to Him.

Lord, as I ask for godly influence to fireproof my marriage, I choose to...

__ *Love my spouse by...*

__ *Obey God by...*

__ *Value my marriage by...*

__ *Express these truths by...*

A Prayer for Pursuing God

Father God,
I am so often tempted to act rather than pray!
Forgive me for the busy, distracted life that I often live outside the
bounds of your Word and Your voice.
I choose today, to seek You first.

First before self-saving actions
First before urgent voices that pull me out of Your presence
First before the opinions of others
First before my hunger to be seen or admired.

I declare Your Word as faithful and true. You are my foundation,
my light, my direction, and my hope. Help us to quit making our
marriage about us. It's all about You. Amen.

Living the Love Dare This Week

We challenge you to pray with your spouse tonight
before going to bed. Pray about the three items each
of you shared during this session. Then make this a
new habit in your marriage!

This week in *The Love Dare* you'll be experiencing
your way through days 31-35. As we approach the
end of an incredible journey, remember that day 43
is just as important as day 1.

Establishing a Covenant Marriage

Marriage is holy matrimony, a covenant
relationship in which God is glorified.
When your wedding vows are expressed
to Him as well as to one another,
your marriage honors God and
is a testimony to others.

Ignite

In marriage we learn a lot about each other through the daily activities of living.

> 1. **Share a few "unwritten rules" in your marriage. Is there a story behind any of them?**
>
>
> **What is the most serious contract you ever signed?**

YOUR LOVE DARES IN ACTION

As you live out the principles in Days 31-35 of *The Love Dare*, you continue to lead your heart to forgive and honor and unconditionally love your spouse.

> 2. **So far, which dare has had the greatest positive impact on you and your marriage? Share with your group.**
>
> **What characteristics of Christlike behavior did you observe and affirm in your mate this week?**
>
> **How are you relying more on your spouse's input and concerns as together you face critical decisions together?**

Gear Up

ENGAGING IN RELEVANT SCRIPTURE STUDY

We live in a world of prenuptials, starter wives, and no-fault divorces where marriage is viewed as just a piece of paper, a contract. By definition, a *contract* is a means of setting legal accountability and limited liability; of making certain that first and foremost our own issues are addressed, and of ensuring that someone adheres to certain minimum requirements. A contract must be in writing because it is built around distrust and can be broken by mutual consent.

3. What dangers do you see in a applying a contract-making mentality to your marriage?

Have you ever had to break a contract?

Throughout history, God has initiated loving, trusting, permanent relationships with His people. He makes verbal promises called *covenants* for our good—promises He has never broken and will never break. Our God is a covenant-making God.

In the margin note some examples of biblical covenants. Have you ever noticed how a covenant is often marked by some type of symbol (circumcision, a rainbow, Jesus' cup and bread)?

COVENANTS

NOAH: God would never again destroy all humanity by flood.

ABRAHAM: An entire nation would come from his descendants.

MOSES: Israel would be God's special people.

DAVID: A ruler would sit on his throne forever and the Messiah would come from his lineage.

NEW COVENANT: Jesus' blood provides forgiveness and eternal life to those who believe.

MOVIE MOMENTS
Watch FIREPROOF
clip 10, "Renewing Vows."
Debrief with
activity 5.

4. **What symbol do we normally associate with the marriage covenant? Why do you think that is?**

5. **How do you think this renewal of wedding vows was different from the vows Caleb and Catherine exchanged to start their marriage?**

"¹³(God) no longer respects your offerings or receives them gladly from your hands. ¹⁴Yet you ask, 'For what reason?' Because the Lord has been a witness between you and the wife of your youth. You have acted treacherously against her, though she was your marriage partner and your wife by covenant."

MALACHI 2:13-14, HCSB

Read Malachi 2:13-14 (margin). What do you think it means that God is "a witness" to our vows? What difference does that make?

Intentionally or not, even the act of writing our own vows is evidence to the fact that we have begun to define marriage in our own terms. For God to "witness" our vows (Mal. 2:14), means that the vows we make to our spouse, we are also making to God. We are creating a covenant between ourselves, God, and our spouse that is not to be broken—ever.

A LIFELONG COVENANT MARRIAGE MEANS …

Lifelong Companionship

The marriage relationship is a gift that offers rich, deep, and meaningful companionship for a lifetime (Gen. 2:22-24).

6. **How do you think this kind of companionship compares to simply enjoying time together?**

What do Jesus' words in Matthew 19:6 (margin) indicate about the nature of the bond between a husband and wife?

Lifelong Support

"Two are better than one, because they have a good return for their work: If one falls down, his friend can help him up. But pity the man who falls and has no one to help him up!"
Ecclesiastes 4:9-10, NIV

7. **How have you experienced or observed other couples experiencing the support of which Ecclesiastes 4:9-10 speaks?**

"²²Then the LORD God made the rib He had taken from the man into a woman and brought her to the man. ²³And the man said: This one, at last, is bone of my bone, and flesh of my flesh; this one will be called woman, for she was taken from man. ²⁴This is why a man leaves his father and mother and bonds with his wife, and they become one flesh."

GENESIS 2:22-24, HCSB

"So they are no longer two, but one flesh. What therefore God has joined together, let no man separate."

MATTHEW 19:6, NASB

What is God seeking in the following verse?
"Has not the LORD made them one? In flesh and spirit they are his. And why one? Because he was seeking godly offspring. So guard yourself in your spirit, and do not break faith with the wife of your youth." *Malachi 2:15*, NIV

**MARRIAGE
VOWS ARE …**
Premeditated
Publicly spoken
Witnessed by others

Covenant marriage doesn't just provide support for each spouse, but also for children. God's plan for procreation is within the one-flesh, for-a-lifetime covenant of marriage.

How can husbands and wives support each other in:

Child-rearing   **Spiritual Intimacy**

Vocation   **Finances**

Health   **Forgiveness**

Habits/Addictions   **Lifelong Strength**

8. Can you recall a time you were stumbling through difficult circumstances and your spouse was able to encourage you, "warm you," or even battle on your behalf as Ecclesiastes 4:11-12 mentions?

"¹¹Also, if two lie down together, they will keep warm. But how can one keep warm alone? ¹²Though one may be overpowered, two can defend themselves. A cord of three strands is not quickly broken.

ECCLESIASTES 4:11-12, NIV

Lifelong Accountability

"Therefore, I urge you, brothers, in view of God's mercy, to offer your bodies as living sacrifices, holy and pleasing to God—this is your spiritual act of worship. Do not conform any longer to the pattern of this world, but be transformed by the renewing of your mind. Then you will be able to test and approve what God's will is—his good, pleasing and perfect will." *Romans 12:1-2, NIV*

MARRIAGE VOWS ARE …
Legally binding
Spiritually binding
Physically binding

9. According to Paul's challenge in Romans 12, how do you think the big picture of following Jesus is enhanced by covenant marriage?

"⁵Your attitude should be the same as that of Christ Jesus: ⁶Who, being in very nature God, did not consider equality with God something to be grasped, ⁷but made himself nothing, taking the very nature of a servant, being made in human likeness."

PHILIPPIANS 2:5-7, NIV

Can you recall a circumstance when your spouse helped you maintain an attitude of servanthood, as described in Philippians 2:5-7?

Firefighting

COMPELLING COUPLES TO TRANSFORM THEIR MARRIAGES

"And rejoice in the wife of your youth … Let her … satisfy you at all times; Be exhilarated always with her love."

PROVERBS 5:18-19, NASB

John 10:10 tells us that while the thief comes to kill, steal, and destroy, Jesus comes so we might have life abundant.

10. Take a moment to list ways the thief (Satan) can kill, steal, and destroy the covenant of marriage.

What do you think abundant life might look like in a covenant marriage?

"God … richly provides us with all things to enjoy."

1 TIMOTHY 6:17, HCSB

Marriage should be fun! Covenant marriage takes that joy to even deeper, more enriching dimensions. The relationship Caleb and Catherine discovered is characterized by both transformation and surrender.

"Make my joy complete by being like-minded, having the same love, being one in spirit and purpose."

PHILIPPIANS 2:2, NIV

Husbands: What would happen in your marriage if you devoted yourself to loving, honoring, and serving your wife in all things?

Wives: What would happen if you made it your mission to do everything possible to promote togetherness of heart with your husband? (*The Love Dare*, p. 148)

When couples live out their marriage this way, it is truly holy matrimony. Scripture teaches that covenant marriage is a clear picture of the relationship of God the Father to God the Son and of Christ to his bride, the church (1 Cor. 11:3; Eph. 5:22-25).

Fireproof Now

COMMITTING THROUGH REFLECTION AND PRAYER

---

11. In what ways can you picture your marriage becoming a testimony to others?

When your covenant vows are vertical, expressed to God as well as to your spouse, then your marriage becomes a testimony to the world of the glory of God. .

Lord, as I ask for godly influence to fireproof my marriage, I choose to …

___ *Love my spouse by …*

___ *Obey God by …*

___ *Value my marriage by …*

___ *Express these truths by …*

A Prayer for Covenant Marriage

Father God,
We are a group that wants to follow You
in authentic relationships and covenant.
We need You to sharpen our vision and restore
the brokenness we encounter deep within our spirits.

We need the unity that only You can bring.
We need to follow You with unswerving loyalty
so we are asking for Your strength and the
transformation that is offered in Your world.

Without You, how can we promise anything?
We are desperately dependent on You.

Give us passion and strength to fireproof our marriages
In the name of Jesus, Amen.

Catherine:
 "So what day are
  you on?"
Caleb:
 "43."
Catherine:
 "There are only 40."
Caleb:
 "Who says I have
  to stop?"

KEEPING THE LOVE DARE ALIVE

Who says you
have to stop?

Prepare for a life-changing experience of the
reaffirmation of your vows to each other and to
God. Create or participate in an experience you
will treasure forever.

**Finish this group process by completing your
readings and love dares for days 36-40.**

Leading a Small Group

1. Remember, as a leader, you can never transform a life. You must lead your group into the power of redemptive community, trusting the Holy Spirit to transform lives along the way.

2. The meeting should feel like a conversation, not a classroom experience. Be careful not to say something like, "Now we're going to answer the 'Gear Up' questions."

3. Remember, a great group leader talks less than 10 percent of the time. So don't be afraid of silence. If you create an environment where you fill the gaps of silence, the group will quickly learn they need not join in the conversation.

4. Every group has individuals who can tend to dominate the conversation. This is unhealthy for the group and frustrating to members. As the leader, try to deal with this assertively yet politely. Say something like, "Thanks, Scott, for your thoughts. Now let's hear from someone we haven't heard from yet."

5. Each session contains more material than you can possibly use in an hour. You may want to pick and choose those questions or activities that you feel are most important or simply extend your meeting time to an hour and a half. Whatever your choice, be certain that you value your attendees' time.

6. Be sensitive to the Holy Spirit's leading on issues that need more time. Remember, people and their needs are far more important than completing all the questions.

The Love Dare Bible Study

Leader Guide

- Consider launching your Love Dare experience by watching the FIREPROOF movie as a group in a home. Conclude your study with a covenant-renewal event. (See the CD-ROM for ideas.)
- In a church or other large-group setting, consider round tables for small groups, with a couple to guide each one. Do some activities as a total group.
- Interactive activities are **boldface** and numbered. If you do not have time for all parts, only use the main question.
- At times you may choose to group men and women separately for an activity or do the activity as couples.
- While time frames are suggested in this leader guide, establish the best schedule for your group. If only one hour is available, try to at least extend sessions 1 and 8 to allow special touches (refreshments, evaluation, and so forth).

Small-Group Format

1. IGNITE: *Icebreaker*
2. LOVE DARE REVIEW
3. GEAR UP: *Introduce Topic/Bible Study*
4. FIREFIGHTING: *Helping Couples Transform Their Marriages*
5. FIREPROOF NOW: *Commitments/Wrap-up/Prayer*

Session 1

IGNITE (10 MIN.)

Enthusiastically welcome the group to the Love Dare Bible study. Introduce yourself and small-group leaders. Distribute *The Love Dare Bible Study* books.

Use icebreakers to build community and help couples to get better acquainted. Keep **activity 1** lighthearted and fun.

With the total group, emphasize: *You are being dared to think differently.* Overview the Group Covenant (p. 6) and describe how everything shared in this group will remain confidential.

As an **option** to *Describe a time you followed your heart and regretted it later,* give your own example. The group may not yet be ready to share at that level.

Hand out *The Love Dare* journals. Briefly discuss the format and how future sessions will have review time.

GEAR UP (15-20 MIN.)

Set up the FIREPROOF movie if your group has not viewed it together. **Movie Moments** provide a means to examine biblical themes and issues and incorporate them into our own relationships.

Clip 1 ("For Better or for Worse") highlights ways people think about love. The salt and pepper metaphor is powerful (Salt and pepper are always distinctive with unique purposes = God's plan from creation). Michael's gluing the shakers together introduces covenant marriage and the permanence of vows.

Help couples examine their relationships by looking at what they treasure. Use Scriptures and **clip 2 ("Lead Your Heart")** to make the distinction between following your heart and leading it.

FIREFIGHTING (15 MIN.)
Ask a volunteer to read Psalm 139:23 aloud. Guide the group to personalize ways to guard their hearts and focus on leading their hearts toward God.

FIREPROOF NOW (10 MIN.)
Each week a printed prayer captures the commitments being made. As you conclude, pray for transformed hearts.

If you prefer, develop your own prayer or suggest couples do so. The point is to focus on God and His power. Make sure spouses pray for each other and for couples in the group.

LOVE DARE READINGS
Conclude: *As you begin Love Dare readings 1-5, you will discover more what it means to practically live out leadership of your heart. Dare to build a new discipline. Take the dare!* Highlight Appendix 4 and Introduction.

Session 2

This session continues to focus on leading the heart, as the group examines both positive and negative influences.

In advance, secure two roses and let one wilt (or microwave it for a minute.) Place both roses in a vase.

IGNITE (10 MIN.)
Welcome returning members and involve newcomers in small groups.

Option: Write **activity 1** questions on a dry-erase board. As members arrive, ask them to write responses on index cards. Play "Hot Potato." The person with the hot potato must answer a question.

LOVE DARE REVIEW (10 MIN.)
Devote extra time to review since this is the first week of readings. Use "Power Truths from *The Love Dare*" to help. Sharing a personal story of your journey is a good way to encourage your group.

GEAR UP (15 MIN.)
Show the two roses and comment: *It's more than hard—it's impossible—to grow a rose in a house fire!* Continuing the firefighting motif, move to **activity 3** questions.

Use **clip 3 ("He Said, She Said/ Phone Call")** with **activity 4** to contrast pressures from society with godly support. Other movie themes that may come up are miscommunication/impact of words/gossip; respect; male and female differences.

Prior to **activity 8**, ask a volunteer to read Genesis 3:1-6 aloud. Encourage your group to spend some time assessing how negative influences slowly erode a marriage. If you choose, play softly a song used in the movie (*Casting Crowns*, "Slow Fade").

Remind the group how they lead their heart by replacing negative influences with godly ones.

FIREFIGHTING (15 Min.)
Invite couples to discuss the **Couple Questions** together.

FIREPROOF NOW (10 Min.)
Introduce the LOVE acrostic as a way to express marriage commitments (**activity 9**). Explain: *You will begin building your own LOVE acrostic during this Bible study.* Invite the couples to gather in a circle and pray silently for godly influences as you direct them through this acrostic.

LOVE DARE READINGS
Encourage: *Join God in His work to strengthen your marriage. Live the dare! Read and do Days 6-10.*

Session 3

Place a sports award, plaque, or other recognition in a visible part of the room.

IGNITE (10 MIN.)
Share a picture of yourself as a child or high-school student. Be ready to indicate someone you admired as a child.

LOVE DARE REVIEW (5 MIN.)
Ask a couple to read the modern descriptors of love, alternating statements.

Debrief using one ore more questions in **activity 2** with "Power Truths from *The Love Dare*." As you discuss how this week went, avoid the temptation to send your group on a guilt trip!

GEAR UP (20 MIN.)
Be sensitive to the intense impact of **clip 4**, "The Big Fight." Be prepared to respond to thoughts and emotions.

Enlist three volunteers to read a statement at the appropriate time or prepare visuals.

Ask volunteer 1 to read *Honor defined: Treating someone or something as rare or special*; follow with **activity 3**.

Ask volunteer 2 to read "*A man is about as big as the things that make him angry*" (Winston Churchill). Then watch **clip 4** and do **activity 4**. Talk about how the rules of honor were totally destroyed in this scene.

Clip 5 communicates how disappointment can creep into a relationship. Using Scripture and **activity 6**, guide couples to examine how thoughts, words, and actions often expressed flippantly or cynically can play a part. Allow couples quality time with **activity 7**.

FIREFIGHTING (15 Min.)

Honor and respect play into how a couple handles conflict (**activities 9 and 10**). Before activity 10, call on volunteer 3 to read from day 15, *The Love Dare*: "*To say your mate should be "holy" to you doesn't mean he or she is perfect. ... A person who has become holy to you has a place no one can rival in your heart.*"

Help couples begin writing their own LOVE acrostic.

FIREPROOF NOW (10 MIN.)

Remind couples: *If you are cherishing your spouse, you are honoring Christ!* Close with prayer for a servant heart.

LOVE DARE READINGS

Remind: The Love Dare *is a book to be experienced. That is the way it works!*

Session 4

IGNITE (10 MIN.) Enjoy this time!

LOVE DARE REVIEW (5 MIN.)

To review, use the questions in **activity 2** and "Power Truths from *The Love Dare*."

GEAR UP (20 MIN.)

Encourage group members to share ways they have cleared up misunderstandings/false assumptions in their marriages. Discuss **activities 4-6** in light of **movie clip 6** and Mark 1:40-45.

Option: Develop an "Emotional Safety Meter." Have couples evaluate (1 *not at all*, 10 *completely*) the extent to which their spouse: *Trusts Me with His/Her Heart; Feels Emotionally Safe with Me; Shares His/Her Genuine Feelings and Needs; Shares His/Her Secrets with Me; Knows I Won't Humiliate or Reject Him/Her.*

FIREFIGHTING (15 Min.)

Activities 7-10 help couples learn about, listen to, and respect their spouses.

FIREPROOF NOW (10 MIN.)

Allow couples to continue completing their own LOVE acrostic.

LOVE DARE READINGS

Highlight Appendix 2, "20 Questions for Your Spouse."

Session 5

IGNITE (10 MIN.)

Without comment, hand each person a small gift as he or she enters. Everyone should be given a gift of the same value without having to ask for it.

LOVE DARE REVIEW (5 MIN.)

To review, use the questions in **activity 2** and "Power Truths from *The Love Dare*." Group responses during this review can also be helpful in session 7.

Discuss modern examples of unconditional love. Ask the group to share times they have seen it expressed.

GEAR UP (20 MIN.)

Set up Movie Moments **clip 7** and supporting activities: Caleb has been doing *The Love Dare* for 20 days and he's about ready to toss the entire thing because Catherine is so unresponsive.

Emphasize how Caleb's question "How am I supposed to show love to someone over and over and over again who consistently rejects me?" depicts the depth of God's love to us. Highlight ways the cross changes our perspective.

During this session, watch for signs of conviction from anyone who is not be a Christian. Be available to talk.

Allow couples quality time to unpack **activities 7** and **8**.

FIREFIGHTING (15 Min.)

Activity 9 can help couples see how each spouse sacrifices and serves in the marriage, out of the unconditional love that only comes from God.

FIREPROOF NOW (5 MIN.)

Allow couples to spend time on their LOVE acrostics as they discover ways to take unconditional love home. They can make new commitments or reaffirm earlier ones.

Facilitate a time of worship and praise to conclude. Consider singing several familiar songs *a cappella*. Ask two or three people to voice prayers, thanking God for the cross.

LOVE DARE READINGS

Challenge: *Get out of your spiritual comfort zones next week with days 21-25! Watch what God will do!*

Session 6

As the group enters, have music playing. Choose songs with lyrics about being sorry or apologizing.

IGNITE (10 MIN.)

Continue to enjoy building community as you move into this serious subject.

LOVE DARE REVIEW (5 MIN.)

To review, use questions in **activity 2** and "Power Truths from *The Love Dare*."

Encourage them to share experiences representing issues they have worked out as a couple.

Discuss this statement: "Great marriages don't happen because couples completely stop sinning and failing one another. They happen because couples learn to never stop apologizing and forgiving one another."

GEAR UP (20 MIN.)

The apology scene, **clip 8**, sets up the attitude of true sorrow and forgiveness in contrast to forced apology. Exploring the difference in Caleb from earlier scenes to this one should enable some couples to see their relationship in a different light. The contrast will also be dramatic as you contrast forgiveness with unforgiveness.

(If available, use an X-ray of a broken bone as an object lesson: If something is broken, no matter how painful it is, it must be set or it will not heal properly. The entire body is affected.)

Emphasize answers to, "What Does It Mean to Truly Forgive Someone?"

FIREFIGHTING (15 Min.)

Allow couples time to assess practical ways to lead their hearts to apply forgiveness in their marriages, using **activity 9**.

FIREPROOF NOW (5 MIN.)

You may want couples to unpack the printed prayer for some additional insights into forgiveness.

LOVE DARE READINGS

Encourage the group to continuing praying for each other during the week. Dismiss: *This week take the dare to express your love in a tangible way to your spouse!*

Session 7

Option: In advance, invite couples to bring a favorite dessert to this session.

IGNITE (10 MIN.)

Encourage couples to share in ways that are comfortable for both husband and wife. Build on the fun as you transition to a heavy week of love dares.

Goals are for this session are for couples to: (1) begin praying for and with one another; and (2) start building their marriage on God's Word and submitting each area of their marriage/family to the Word of God.

LOVE DARE REVIEW (5 MIN.)

To review, use the questions in **activity 2** and "Power Truths from *The Love Dare*." Affirm couples as they grapple with some tough issues.

GEAR UP (20 MIN.)

Vary your teaching by asking an animated couple to present the drama sketch (**p. 67**), to set up the group's focus on prayer. Don't assume everyone knows what prayer is or how to pray.

Clip 9 illustrates Caleb's heartfelt prayer: of need and surrender to God, for Catherine to be saved, and for nothing he did to stand in the way. Engage couples in considering why they should pray and what can happen when they pray for each other and for other people (**activity 4**).

You may want to give each couple a rock and a zip-lock bag of sand as they examine Matthew 7:24-27 (**activity 5**). Highlight: *Jesus addresses two foundations for life: the secular view and the life based on God's truths in the Bible and in prayer.*

Move into a look at the role of God's Word in marriage (**activity 6**). Allow adequate time for couple questions.

FIREFIGHTING (15 MIN.)

Encourage couples to take the Test of Family Influences as spouses and to discuss their answers together. Debrief as a total group.

FIREPROOF NOW (5 MIN.)

Couples may want to write their commitments (LOVE acrostic) to each other based on what they hope to apply from this session.

Announce plans for the concluding session.

LOVE DARE READINGS

Encourage couples to begin praying for each other each day, if they do not already do so. Draw attention to Appendices 1 and 3, *The Love Dare*, as offering additional content for this session.

Session 8

Use Day 40 in your preparation. You may want to allow more time for this session. Gather items for Gear Up in advance.

Ignite (10 min.)
Prepare to share some rules developed over time in your marriage. If funny, share a story but keep the group on task.

Love Dare Review (5 min.)
To review, use **activity 2** questions and "Power Truths from *The Love Dare*." Allow a few couples to share their most meaningful dare.

Gear Up (20 min.)
Bring a wedding photo and a legal document. Briefly talk about how these agreements differ. Move into differences between contract and covenant, including biblical covenants.

Use **clip 10** and **activity 5** to examine the difference God makes in our marriages. Involve couples in examining the lifelong impact and benefits of a covenant marriage (**activities 6-9**).

Firefighting (15 min.)
Use **activity 7, part 3** and **activity 10** to help couples make day-to-day applications. **Option**: Invite couples to write Ten Commandments for their marriage, to build a hedge of protection around it. Like the biblical Ten Commandments, some statements should address their relationship with God. Other statements should center on their relationship with each other and other people.

Fireproof Now (10 min.)
Ask individuals to develop their LOVE acrostic as both a commitment and an action plan. Invite individuals, couples, or subgroups to share some commitments with the entire group. Ask the group to continue to pray for and to support each other.

Prepare your group for the incredible experience of reaffirmation to covenant marriage that is planned (hopefully, next Sunday). Explain: *This event will not only be meaningful for those of you renewing your vows, it will also act as a powerful testimony to those who witness it.*

Love Dare Readings
Encourage: *Like Caleb, don't stop now, as some of the most enriching dares come after this session, with love dares 36-40.*

Celebrate the friendships you have made and the steps you have taken. Stay in touch with each other or otherwise help each other remain accountable to strengthen your marriage. Indicate your willingness to remain a part of their lives.

Newlyweds can travel anywhere in the world for their honeymoon.

But where should they go when it's over?

The LifeWay marriage site offers a variety of resources to help keep relationships going and growing. Discover books and Bible studies. Peruse magazine articles or respond to our new blog. And sign up for newsletters or a weekend event. Visit us today and see why our site is a favorite destination for married couples.

www.lifeway.com/marriage

LifeWay | Adults

Two Ways to Earn Credit
for Studying LifeWay Christian Resources Material

Christian Growth Study Plan resources are available for course credit for personal growth and church leadership training.

Courses are designed as plans for personal spiritual growth and for training current and future church leaders. To receive credit, complete the book, material, or activity. Respond to the learning activities or attend group sessions, when applicable, and show your work to your pastor, staff member, or church leader. Then go to *www.lifeway.com/CGSP,* or call the toll-free number for instructions for receiving credit and your certificate of completion.

CONTACT INFORMATION:
Christian Growth Study Plan
One LifeWay Plaza, MSN 117
Nashville, TN 37234
CGSP info line 1-800-968-5519
www.lifeway.com/CGSP
To order resources 1-800-485-2772

For information about studies in the Christian Growth Study Plan, refer to the current catalog online at the CGSP Web address. This program and certificate are free LifeWay services to you.

Need a CEU?

Receive Continuing Education Units (CEUs) when you complete group Bible studies by your favorite LifeWay authors.

CONTACT INFORMATION:
CEU Coordinator
One LifeWay Plaza, MSN 150
Nashville, TN 37234
Info line 1-800-968-5519
www.lifeway.com/CEU

Some studies are approved by the Association of Christian Schools International (ACSI) for CEU credits. Do you need to renew your Christian school teaching certificate? Gather a group of teachers or neighbors and complete one of the approved studies. Then go to *www.lifeway.com/CEU* to submit a request form or to find a list of ACSI-approved LifeWay studies and conferences. Book studies must be completed in a group setting. Online courses approved for ACSI credit are also noted on the course list. The administrative cost of each CEU certificate is only $10 per course.